# MYSTERIES
## OF THE ANCIENT WORLD

# CLOUD CITIES
# OF THE INKA

### KAREN WISE

WEIDENFELD & NICOLSON
LONDON

*View of the Inka ruins of Machu Picchu, one of the most famous archaeological sites in the New World. The beauty, setting and aura of mystery surrounding the site continue to fascinate visitors from around the world.*

The year is 1532. A group of fewer than 200 Spanish soldier-explorers, accompanied by a few Catholic priests, arrive on the north coast of what is now Peru. Disembarking, they begin a journey of discovery and destruction that will end in the

downfall of an empire that covers much of western South America. In their quest for gold and glory, the Spanish colonists, or *conquistadores*, take over the huge and efficient government of the Inka, changing the course not only of American but also of European history.

The great empire of the Inka had been built quickly, during the 100 years before the arrival of the Spanish. By the time of European contact, the Inka had annexed an area larger than even the great Roman empire. Even more amazing, the Inka empire covered some of the roughest terrain on earth, including desert, the steep mountains of the Andes range, and dense jungles. Without the wheel, and lacking any animal that could be ridden, the Inka were able to move huge numbers of men and resources quickly across vast expanses of varied lands. They amassed great wealth and kept strict accounts without writing as we know it. Where did this great empire come from? How was it ruled? And how could a few Spaniards conquer it so quickly?

## *The Origins of the Empire*

The Inka empire emerged after thousands of years of cultural development in the Andes. The Inka harnessed technology, economic, social, political and religious practices that had grown from the deserts, mountains and even the jungles of South America to control vast territories and huge populations during the 15th and 16th centuries AD. The Inka modified everything from farming practices to religious rituals to suit their aims, and reinforced their legitimacy by re-telling history to emphasize their own civilization over those that had preceded them.

Characteristically, the Inka tale of their own origins emphasized Inka divine right as well as their civilizing influence on the surrounding peoples. One version of the Inka origin story was written by the Spanish colonial chronicler Bernabé Cobo in the early 17th century:

*Pottery vessel in the form of a man playing the flute. During the Inka period, regional pottery styles from coastal and highland areas continued to be used, as in this piece.*

*There came forth from a cave ... Pacarictampu ... four brothers called Manco Capac,*
*Ayar Chache, Ayar Uchi and Agay Manco; and with them four sisters of theirs, who were*
*called Mama Huaco, Mama Ocllo, Mama Ragua and Mama Cura ... With the seeds*
*of maize and other foods that the Creator gave them, they set off on the road to the Valley*
*of Cuzco ... They came to a high hill called the Hanacauri (which afterwards was a*
*famous place of worship among the Indians because this fable took place there) and from*
*there the eldest brother marked the land, and, hurling four slingstones towards the four*
*corners of the earth, he took possession of it ... one of the brothers returned to*
*Pacarictampu, entered the cave ... and remained there without ever appearing again; of*
*the three that remained, two of them turn themselves into stones. . . thus only Manco*
*Capac arrived with his four sisters at the site where the city of Cuzco is located now. There*
*Manco Capac made friends little by little with the natives of the region, who were few in*
*number and lived spread out over that valley like savages without order or harmony. With*

*The great stone blocks making up the walls at the Inka fortress of Sacsahuaman, on the outskirts of Cuzco, support a series of terraces and open spaces where the modern-day descendants of the Inka still celebrate Inti Raymi, a festival of the sun.*

*A 19th-century resident of the Cuzco area sitting on the ruins of the Inka city of Ollantaytambo, drawn by E. G. Squier for* **Peru: Travel and Exploration in the land of the Incas** *(1877).*

*The legacy of Inka bridge building was still in evidence when 19th-century archaeological explorer Ephraim Squier visited Peru. His drawing shows details of the use of thick ropes to make sturdy – if not very stable – bridges.*

*the industry and help of his sisters, who called him the son of the Sun and spoke to him with great respect and reverence, especially because he was a peaceful, very prudent and humane man, he came to be respected and obeyed by all.* (Cobo, *History of the Inca Empire*, (Austin, 1979), pp. 103–4)

This was one of the stories the Inka told about themselves. Other evidence, especially from archaeological studies, indicates that the Inka were in no way responsible for bringing either agriculture or civilization to the Andes, although they may eventually have brought relative peace to the Cuzco region. Before their emergence as rulers of an empire, the Inka were the inhabitants of one of many small competing and war-like cities found in the area beginning in the 11th century. Far from civilizing savage peoples, the Inka fought with, and finally conquered, nearby cities inhabited by people much like themselves. They went on, however, to conquer vast territories, and by the mid-16th century had annexed an area that stretched from modern-day Colombia to Chile, and from the desert coast on the west well into the jungles east of the Andean mountain chain. Without horses, the wheel, or writing as we know it, the Inka conquered a territory larger than any then known on earth, developing a vast economy that was efficient at both feeding people and transporting goods.

## Cuzco, the Inka Capital

The imperial city of Cuzco was both the heart and the head of the Inka empire. Located at 3,395 m above sea level, Cuzco is one of the highest capital cities known. Carefully planned and constructed, Cuzco featured a huge central plaza that was surrounded by massive buildings. The city was laid out along a grid pattern (some say in the shape of a puma), and its 4,000 buildings were found in two major sectors, known as upper and lower Cuzco. Inka Cuzco was a splendid city, and many of its buildings were built of cut and dressed stone that was fitted together so precisely that no mortar was needed.

*The Spanish razed much of Inka Cuzco and built their colonial town on top of it, but the legacy of the Inka is visible everywhere in the finely cut and dressed stone. Squier captured the feel of 19th-century Cuzco with this drawing of an Inka doorway.*

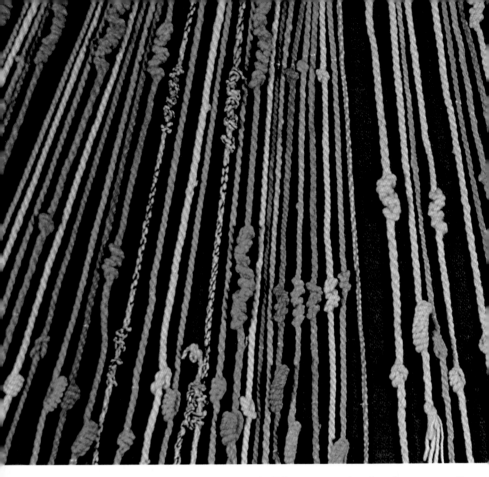

The walls of many of the important buildings were painted and some were finished with gold and silver.

In Inka geography, Cuzco was the hub of the empire, with both secular and sacred lines and roads leading out from its centre. The empire was known as Tawantinsuyu, or the Land of the Four Quarters, and the kingdom was divided into four sections for administrative purposes. Each of the four quarters had a governor. Inka administration was hierarchical, with local leaders at the base and a series of administrators overseeing the local leaders, particularly ensuring that each group provided the Inka with the labour and goods they owed to the Inka.

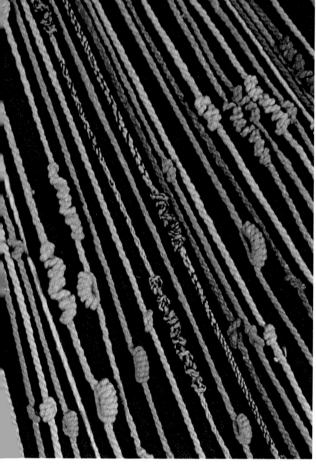

*A* quipu *knotted string recording device.* Quipu *were made and used by trained scribes who were part of the extensive bureaucracy of the Inka empire.*

The task of keeping track of the goods that flowed in and out of Inka storehouses and of all other aspects of Inka activities was a huge job. It is hard to understand how the Inka managed it without a system of writing (symbolic representation of spoken language). What they did have was an extraordinary method of record-keeping using groups of knotted string, known as *quipu*, which were made and read by trained specialists. *Quipu* were made of long cords of coloured string, and knots and groups of knots placed at specific intervals represented numbers in the decimal system. Because the *quipu* are so different from European writing, most of the Spanish do not seem to have recognized them for what they were, native records of the empire, and many

were destroyed. Those that remain in museums around the world continue to intrigue researchers, who try to understand how this system, so different from our own, was used.

Transportation was critical in the ancient empire, just as it is today. The Inka built a huge network of roads that ran the length and width of the empire, linking Cuzco with major and minor regional capitals, administrative centres, outposts and religious pilgrimage sites. The Inka road system covered more than 25,000 km, and perhaps as much as 40,000 km. Road construction varied, depending on terrain, and could include huge stone stairways and long bridges where necessary. On important roads, way-stations that included store-houses for food and other important state resources were found about a day's walk from one another. The wheel was not used by the Inka, and they had no

*The Inkas combined stone carving, masonry and natural rock in settings such as Machu Picchu.*

*Painted wood ceremonial vase (kero) showing a man hunting llamas. Keros were used to drink chicha (corn beer) at all ceremonial, civic and festive occasions.*

13

animal such as the horse that could be ridden; they did, however, have the llama, a small South American relative of the camel that was used as a pack animal as well as for meat. Huge caravans of llamas carried goods across the empire. In addition, runners, known as *chaski*, could wait at way-stations along the Inka roads, from which they ran relay-style to deliver messages and even goods to the Inka.

## *How the Inka Conquered the Andes*

Pre-Inka Peru was dominated by many small local states, as well as by a few larger and more important regional states, such as the Chimu empire on the north coast of Peru. As the Inka came to rule the areas around Cuzco in the early 15th century, they began to develop some of the traits that would characterize them as the empire grew. Distinctive pottery and clothing were developed and the Inka began to codify the rules and customs that were to dominate the Andean world for the next century. They developed a sumptuary code, including rules prohibiting all but the Inka royalty from wearing certain clothing and symbols, and limiting the use of many titles to descendants of the original Inka towns. The Inka eventually allowed the people from towns surrounding Cuzco to use special titles and wear certain clothes previously limited to the Inka, but they enforced strictly the divisions between people of different towns and regions, as well as different classes.

*A jar in the form of two houses. Pottery forms depicting structures, plants, animals and people were used on pre-Inka and Inka pottery throughout the central Andes, especially in coastal areas.*

15

The Inka first conquered the nearby groups, building a base of power in the Cuzco area over the course of several generations. Then, during the second half of the 15th century, a vast expansion took place, accompanied by military campaigns and incredible logistical feats. The army was marched huge distances to conquer areas ever farther from Cuzco. The soldiers walked, accompanied by huge caravans of llamas, packing provisions as well as porters and other support personnel. The armies were fed from what they brought and

*The Inka used aqueducts in irrigation canals and to bring water to towns and sacred sites. This one, drawn by Squier, appears to have been built or rebuilt under the Spanish.*

*A kero (or ceremonial vase) depicting an Inka nobleman (orejon) in a cape and feather headdress. Depictions on pottery and other artefacts help archaeologists reconstruct ancient patterns of dress and behaviour.*

were also provided for from the vast stores kept in provincial capitals and at roadside way-stations.

As the empire grew, so too did the wealth and power of the Inka. The state used a variety of mechanisms to build infrastructure and to establish itself in each new region that was conquered. When they subdued small states and chiefdoms, they took over the capitals and made them into regional administrative centres. In areas that lacked adequate infrastructure for the needs of the

*F*ine cut-stone
masonry,
trapezoidal niches,
windows and door-
ways are visible at
Machu Picchu.

empire, the Inka constructed new provincial capitals, centralizing regional power. They often constructed new agricultural canals and terraces, modifying and expanding existing productive networks, and installing state storehouses and administrative centres.

Whenever possible, the Inka used the local kings and chiefs to help them take over new regions. If the local rulers co-operated, they received wealth and privilege and were allowed to maintain and even enhance their political power within the local region. Of course, not all local leaders were content to serve the growing Inka state, and those who preferred independence were removed and sometimes dealt with harshly. To prevent rebellion by local leaders, the Inka developed systems of incentives and punishments. The sons of local leaders were taken to Cuzco to be educated in the Inka system. This had two advantages: the young heirs to local leaders would be educated to take over rule of their homelands in the style that best suited the Inka; furthermore, the young heirs kept in Cuzco served as potential hostages in case their fathers or other relatives staged a rebellion against the state.

Local groups who proved especially difficult to subdue were dealt with largely through removal. Although local rebellious leaders might be executed or otherwise punished, their followers would simply be moved to other areas. In the most extreme cases, part or all of a village population was moved from its homes, and replaced with other groups more loyal to the state. People from different towns and regions were suspicious of one another and were likely to report on any illegal activities by their neighbours. Groups of people who were moved by the Inka, especially those who were loyal to the Inka, were often placed in areas of either strategic or economic importance, where they could develop new areas of agricultural productivity and keep watch on less loyal local people.

*K*ero *of painted wood, showing Inka hunting deer in the Amazon forest. The Inka empire covered desert, mountain and jungle regions at the time of the Spaniards' arrival in Peru.*

The Inka built up vast wealth by deploying and developing traditional patterns of community-based labour. Although they exacted tribute in the form of raw materials and finished goods from some areas and in certain circumstances, most of the state's resources were gathered through what is often

*Classic Inka architecture featured trapezoidal doorways set into walls of cut, dressed and precisely placed stone blocks.*

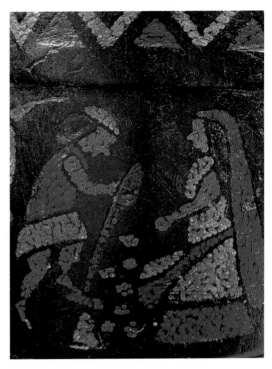

*A kero decorated with a man digging with a taclla, while a woman sows seeds. The Inka empire was based on agriculture and most of its citizens were farmers.*

called a labour tax. Under the most common system, communities provided the state with labour, and each able-bodied male member of the community spent a certain percentage of his time working directly for the state. State-owned agricultural fields and flocks of animals were cared for by members of

each local community. The subjects of the Inka also made cloth for the empire, and worked on state projects, including road and bridge building, and the construction of large buildings. While they worked on state or communal projects, the people were provided with food and with *chicha* beer and coca leaves, and larger projects would be done in a festival atmosphere.

In addition to those who worked part time for the state under the labour tax system, there were also groups of both men and women who worked full time for the state, and who were fed and clothed by the state. The best known group was that of the women known as *mamakuna*. Beautiful young girls from around the kingdom were taken from their homes to live apart in groups of other such women. The *mamakuna* wove cloth, brewed *chicha*, and engaged in religious activities. The Inka controlled the rights to marriage and reproduction of these women, who could be given by the Inka either in marriage or as concubines to favoured kinsmen and regional leaders. There were also men who worked full time for the Inka, mostly as herders, but they could marry as they chose and only their herding activities seem to have been controlled by the state.

Agriculture was one of the mainstays of the Inka economy, and it was intensified and expanded in many areas. Land was divided in a three-tiered system. Local communities controlled much of it, and on these lands most people grew the crops that fed them and their families. There were also lands dedicated to

*The Inka built wide roads across the desert, narrow stairways and paths through mountain passes, and suspension bridges across impassable sections of torrential rivers, like this one, which crossed the Apurimac River in the highlands of Peru, drawn by E. G. Squier.*

*Painted wooden* kero *(overleaf) depicting a woman with flowers.*

25

*S*quiers's illustration of the **intiwatana** of Pisac. *Most important Inka cities probably had enclosed carved stones like this one, but the Spanish destroyed most of them in their attempt to stamp out native religion during the colonial era.*

certain religious shrines, cults and rituals, where community members grew crops and herded animals that were used to support religious activities. State lands were those owned by the Inka, and worked by local people under the labour tax system. From these lands came the stores of food, wool, animals and other goods amassed by the state and kept in state warehouses until needed to support military campaigns or other state needs.

## Religion and Sacrifice

Inka religion was based on allegiance not just to the sun, father of the Inka, but also to moon, stars and earth, as well as to innumerable gods and spirits who inhabited mountains, streams, rocks and other natural features. The gods of the Inka were worshipped in every setting, from the spectacular and monumental Temple of the Sun in Cuzco to tiny shrines found across the empire. Worship included many forms of offerings and sacrifices. Offerings often included such things as *chicha* and coca leaves, as well as items of food and small carved figures. Animals, including domesticated guinea pigs, llamas and alpacas, were also sacrificed, especially at major ceremonies. In some cases, human sacrifices also took place.

Although human sacrifice was not common it was important, and major

*A gold votive figure of a llama. Metalworking in gold, silver and copper was practised throughout the Inka empire. During the early colonial period the Spanish collected as much gold and silver as they could find and shipped it to Spain, and few artefacts such as this one survive.*

*The remote city of Machu Picchu was built on a high peak in the jungle at the edge of the Urubamba, known as the Sacred Valley of the Inkas. Carefully planned and built into the contours of the land, this ruined city may have been some kind of sacred retreat for the Inka ruler.*

ceremonies were held when it occurred. A recent archaeological discovery of a young girl who was sacrificed on a high peak in southern Peru provides some indication of what happened. The girl, a teenager, was fed and drugged, led up a sacred mountain, and there killed with a blow to the head. She was wrapped in fine cloth and her body left as an offering, possibly to the thunder god.

*T*he intiwatana, often called
the 'Hitching Post of the
Sun', may have been used to
observe movements of the sun,
or for sacrifices and ceremonies.

*T*he ruined city of Machu Picchu serves as a monument to Inka architectural and engineering skill, perched dramatically on a mountain peak surrounded by sacred mountains.

## *The Conquest*

One of the most often asked questions about the demise of the Inka empire is how could it have been possible for less than 200 Spanish adventurer-soldiers, many of them illiterate opportunists, to have conquered this powerful empire. The best answer seems to be a combination of luck, disease and technology. In

***The city of Ollantaytambo in Cuzco province, one of the last to built by the Inkas.***

the first place, the Inka seem not to have had a well-established system for succession. They generally had many children, one of whom would be designated as his heir. At the time the Spanish arrived the Inka ruler Huayna Capac had died, as had his designated heir. Another son, Atahualpa, had been fighting for the throne. With his brother dead, possibly of smallpox, which the Europeans

had just introduced to the vulnerable natives, Atahualpa seemed destined to take over as the Inka ruler. The Spanish, however, succeeded in capturing Atahualpa, holding him for a huge ransom of gold and silver, and then killing him.

The Spanish were able to ally themselves with some of the groups that opposed Atahualpa, as well as with other groups who had not been happy under the Inka, and who saw the Spaniards as their chance to escape from the yoke of Inka rule. The Spanish also had guns, which, though slow to load and far less accurate than the bows and spears of the Inka warriors, were novel and certainly loud. Horses, too, may have proved daunting to the natives. It seems most likely, however, that the combination of European diseases, and the circumstances within the young empire itself, provided the most important support for the bands of Spaniards who took over an empire and established what would be hundreds of years of colonial rule.

*The ruins of Inka architecture are everywhere, as shown by Squier in his drawings, such as this one showing two men seated in front of an Inka terrace wall.*

CLOUD
CITIES OF
THE INKA

PHOTOGRAPHIC ACKNOWLEDGEMENTS
Cover E.T. Archive [ETA]; pp. 2–3, 4, 6, 10–11
ETA; p.12 Karen Wise [KW]; pp. 13, 14, 17 ETA;
pp. 18–9 KW; p. 20 ETA; pp. 22–3 KW;
pp. 23, 25–6, 29 ETA; pp. 30–31, 32–3 KW;
pp. 34–5, 36–7 ETA. The illustrations on
pp. 7, 8, 9, 16, 24, 28 and 38 are from
*Peru: Travel and Exploration in the Land of the Incas*
(1877) by E.G. Squiers.

First published in Great Britain 1997
by George Weidenfeld and Nicolson Ltd
The Orion Publishing Group
5 Upper St Martin's Lane
London WC2H 9EA

A CIP catalogue record for this book is available
from the British Library
ISBN 0 297 823175

Picture Research: Joanne King

Designed by Harry Green

Typeset in Baskerville